WITHDRAWN

MANDALAS
to Embroider

First published in 2018

Search Press Limited
Wellwood, North Farm Road,
Tunbridge Wells, Kent TN2 3DR

ISBN: 978-1-78221-544-8

PUBLISHER'S NOTE
The Publishers and author can accept no responsibility for any
consequences arising from the information, advice or instructions
given in this publication.

Readers are permitted to reproduce any of the items in this book for
their personal use, or for the purposes of selling for charity, free of
charge and without the prior permission of the Publishers. Any use
of the items for commercial purposes is not permitted without the
prior permission of the Publishers.

SUPPLIERS
If you have difficulty in obtaining any of the materials and equipment
mentioned in this book, then please visit the Search Press website
for details of suppliers at searchpress.com

For more information about the author and her work, please visit her
blog at carinascraftblog.com and her shop at polkaandbloom.com.
Carina is on Instagram too as @carinacraftblog.

Printed in China through Asia Pacific Offset

Dedication

For Tony.
Love, love, love.

Acknowledgments

It has been a great pleasure to work on this book
with my editors Emily Adam and Katie French, and
everyone at Search Press. Thank you to Cara Ackerman
at DMC UK for providing all the beautiful threads for
the book, and to Sonia Lyne at Dandelyne™ and Nicole
Twena at cloudcraft.co.uk for supplying the Dandelyne
hoops. Props to my wonderful agent, Kate McKean.
Finally, big love to Christine Asbridge for having my
back, and for plying me with vegan chocolate.

MANDALAS
to Embroider

KALEIDOSCOPE STITCHING
IN A HOOP

Search Press

by
Carina Envoldsen-Harris

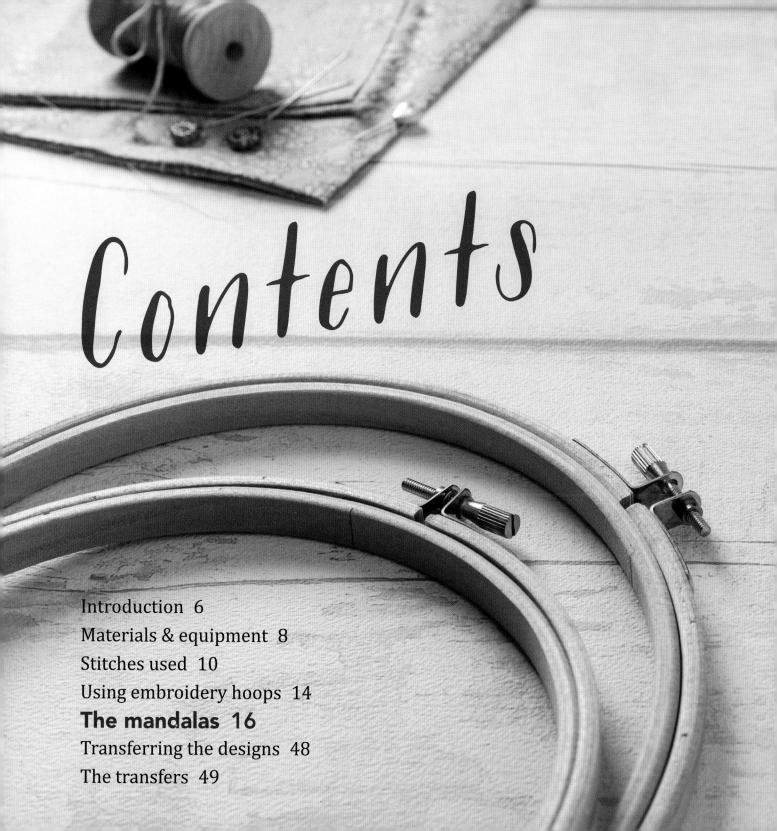

Contents

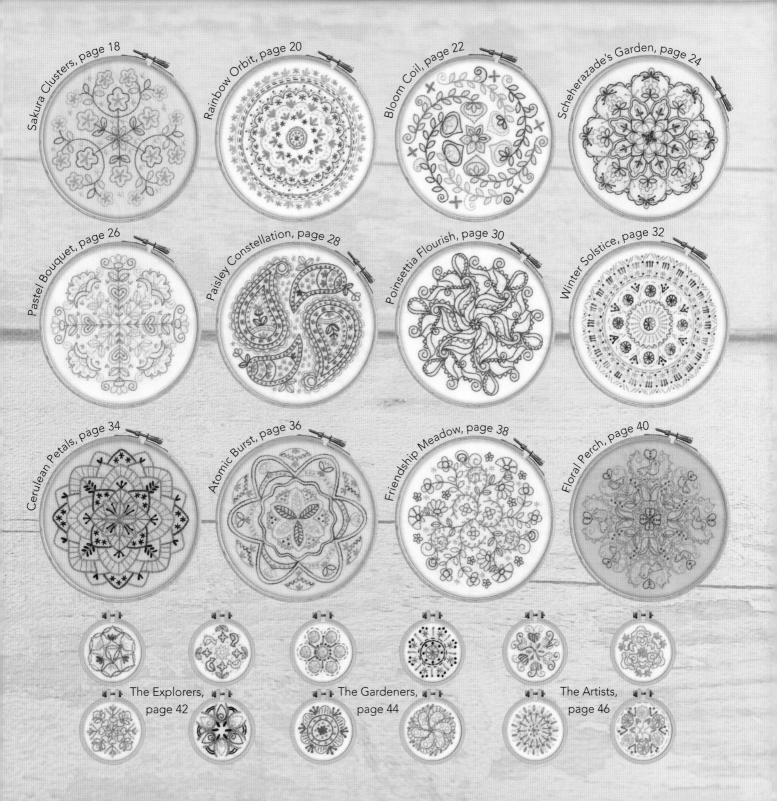

Introduction

Mandala is the Sanskrit word for 'circle'. These days, it is often used as a generic term for a particular motif, especially in arts and crafts, usually with a concentric design or one which radiates from the centre.

The mandala is an important ritual and spiritual symbol in Hinduism and Buddhism, denoting the Universe and the concept of a never-ending life. Different parts of the mandala have different symbolic meanings. The outermost circle is usually a ring of fire which symbolizes transformation and wisdom.

A square structure in the centre is a temple that contains the essence of the Buddha; the temple has four gates which represent several ideas, including the four directions: North, East, South and West.

Ritual mandalas are visual aids for concentration and introversive meditation leading to a greater awareness of the world, physically and spiritually. Famously, Tibetan monks create mandalas with coloured sand over a number of weeks, and then the finished mandala will be destroyed as a lesson on the impermanence of life.

Mandalas have become increasingly popular around the world for less spiritual purposes. They are attractive as a creative outlet and as decoration. The process of drawing a mandala is relaxing and sometimes even meditative.

As well as being a way to embellish cloth, embroidery has those same relaxing and meditative qualities. Sitting quietly and focusing on making stitches on fabric, the mind calms down and the rest of the world melts away for a few minutes or a couple of hours.

In this book you will find a collection of twenty-four mandala-inspired motifs. All the motifs have been stitched as samplers which you can see from pages 18 to 47, and are also provided as detachable, iron-on transfers at the back of the book. With each sampler you will find notes on the colours and stitches used, but they're only there as inspiration – don't be afraid to experiment and pick your own colour and stitch combinations.

You can also use the motifs to embellish pre-made or handmade clothes and accessories. Some ideas are shown on the facing page for inspiration.

If you are new to embroidery, have a look through the sections at the start of the book where you will find instructions for the ten key stitches used in the samplers. You will also find tips for choosing materials, transferring motifs and using a hoop. If a particular stitch is new to you, you may find it useful to practise it on a separate piece of fabric before you dive into a project.

I hope you will enjoy some quiet time spent stitching these mandala motifs as well as the end result, whether you are making them for yourself or for someone else.

Happy stitching!
xo Carina

There are lots of ways you can use these motifs. Embellish clothes: T-shirts, skirts, or even the back of a jacket. Plain tote bags are also excellent canvases for embroidered embellishments.

Perhaps you want to make something from scratch? There is an endless variety of cushion covers to make. Stitch all the large motifs in the same colours and include them in a quilt. The mini mandalas are perfect for adding to a shirt pocket or a phone cover. And of course they can be made into brooches or necklaces using the Dandelyne™ hoops.

Materials & equipment

To get started with embroidery you don't need a lot of fancy gear: gather together some fabric, thread, needles, an embroidery hoop and a pair of scissors and you have all you need.

Needles

For most embroidery, the best needles to use are **embroidery/crewel needles (1)**. They are fine, sharp needles with a large eye. They range from sizes 1–10, and the higher the number, the finer the needle. As a rule of thumb, use the higher numbers on finer fabrics where you will usually use a finer thread, and a lower number for heavier fabrics. Chenille needles are useful for thick threads and milliner's needles are handy when working lots of French knots.

Thread

DMC stranded cotton has been used for the samplers **(2)**. It comes in a lot of colours, is colourfast, and can be divided so that the thickness can be adjusted to the fabric. All the samplers in this book are stitched with two strands of thread. Use a thicker thread with heavier or textured fabrics, otherwise the stitches may disappear into the weave of the fabric. Other brands can be used, as well as other types of thread; for example, silk, perle cotton, crewel wool or sashiko thread. Even yarn for knitting and crochet can be used.

Fabrics

The samplers in the book are stitched on **cotton fabric (see below)** but you can embroider on pretty much anything you can push a needle through – paper, card or even wood. When choosing fabric, bear in mind that not all will work well with the transfers with regard to texture or colour. For the best results, use a light-coloured, even-weave fabric such as cotton or cotton-linen blend.

Thread conditioner

A thread conditioner, such as **Thread Heaven**, is nice to have when you are working with metallic or other special threads **(3)**. It also makes separating thread strands easier and decreases twisting and knotting of the thread.

Hoop

A **hoop** (sometimes referred to as an embroidery frame) keeps the fabric taut so the stitches will be more even and prevents the fabric from puckering too much **(4)**. Hoops are usually wooden, but are also available in plastic. They come in a range of sizes, numbered by their diameter in inches. Use a hoop which is 2.5–5cm (1–2in) larger all around the motif so you won't have to reposition the hoop. Always take the fabric out of the hoop when you know you will not be working on it for a while. Leaving the fabric in the hoop may create permanent marks in the fabric. I have also used special mini hoops by Dandelyne™ **(5)** for displaying the mini designs, and transforming them into jewellery pieces.

Other useful tools

Embroidery scissors (6) Make sure these are always nice and sharp

Water soluble fabric pen (7) For drawing the designs onto the fabric (see page 48)

Rulers or tape measure (8) To measure your fabric pieces for framing

Scalloped edge pinking shears (9) Cuts a pretty rounded edge into your fabric

Fabric scissors (10) For cutting your fabric

Cotton twill binding tape (11) Useful when placing your fabric in the embroidery hoop

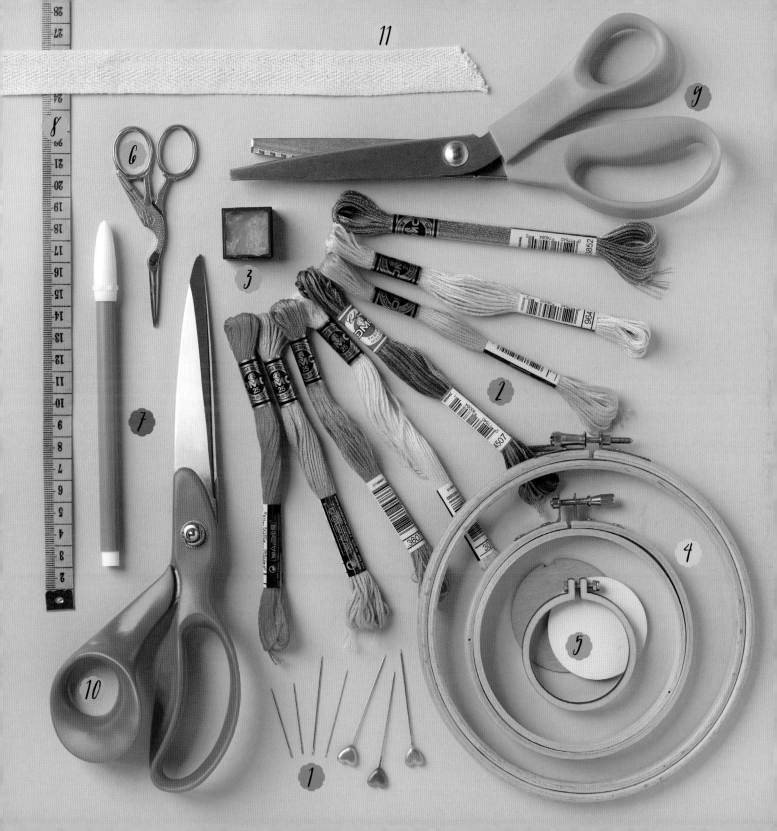

Stitches used

Ten embroidery stitches have been used to create all the motifs in this book. Once you've learnt the stitches, don't be afraid to experiment and try all sorts of stitch combinations when sewing your own mandalas – you'll be amazed by how unique they look when the same design is embroidered with different stitches.

● Starting off your stitch

Thread your needle and make a waste knot. Come in through the front of your work and push your needle through. Come up through the fabric (**1**), approx. 2cm (¾in) away from your starting point, in the direction of your design. You can then continue to work your design (**2**).

● Fastening off your thread

At the end of your design, weave the thread through the stitches at the back of the embroidery and then cut off the end of the thread (**1**). Return to the front, then cut away the waste knot (**2**).

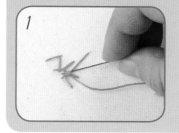 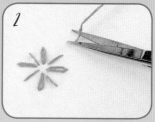

● Back stitch

The most important stitch in the book, it is a gapless stitch used to outline all the mandala motifs.

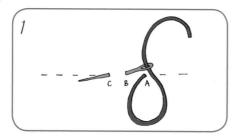 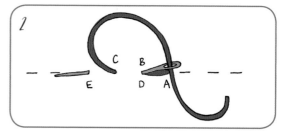

Bring your needle up through the fabric at A, insert your needle into the fabric at B, then along and up again at C.

Take the needle back to B (D), then bring the needle up at E. The gap should be the size of the stitch. Continue to work this way, making sure the stitches are a consistent length. When you finish, thread your needle through the stitches on the wrong side of the fabric.

● *Running stitch*

A simple stitch used for decorative edging. Make sure the length of the stitches – and the spaces in between – are the same each time.

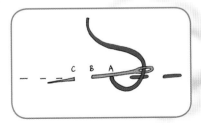

Bring your needle up through the fabric at A, back down at B and then up at C. Continue the rest of the line in this way.

● *Straight stitch*

Used to fill petals and leaves, or when you want to create single stitch lines.

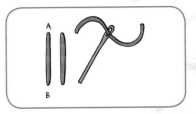

Bring the needle up through at A and down into the fabric at B. If you are working a row of straight stitches, make sure that their length – and the gap in between – are consistent.

● *Chain stitch*

Sewn closely together, this stitch creates bolder outlines.

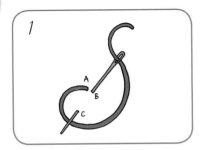

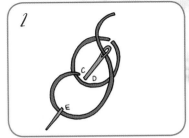

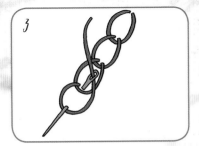

Bring the needle up at A and back down at B, securing a small loop with your thumb.

Bring the needle up at C, so that the needle is on top of the thread. Pull the thread tight to form the first 'link' in the chain.

Make as many stitches as required, making sure they are a consistent in shape and size. Finish the last chain with a small straight stitch.

11

● Star stitch

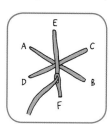

This decorative stitch can be used to fill shapes, or scattered throughout to add pops of colour.

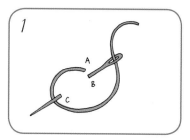

Pull the needle up at A, insert it at B, bring the needle up at C and insert at D to make a flattened cross. Then pull the needle up at E and insert at F to complete the star.

● Lazy daisy

Create lovely little leaves and petals in moments with these five detached chain stitches.

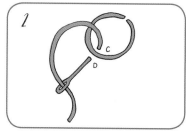

Bring your needle up through the fabric at A and insert it at B, as close to A as possible. Pull the thread gently to make a loop.

Insert the needle at D – make sure you pass the thread over the loop.

Make as many stitches as required, sewing them close together in a circle to form a flower.

● Fly stitch

Little V- or Y-shapes used for decorative edging, as fillers or for spiky petals.

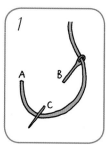

Bring the needle up at A and down at B. Don't pull the thread too tightly to leave a small loop. Bring the needle up at C – where you want your the base of your 'V' or bowl of the 'Y' – and loop it over the stitch you made between A and B.

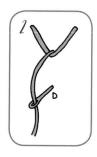

Now pull the thread to tighten the 'V' or 'Y' shape. Take the needle back down to D to make a 'Y'; for the 'V', only take it just below point C, which will then complete the stitch.

French knot & pistil stitch

French knots and pistil stitches are similar, except for pistil stitches you take the needle through the fabric slightly further away from point A. These are used for stamens and as decorative fillers.

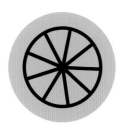

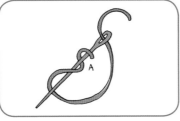

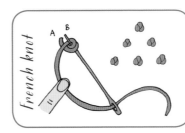

French knot

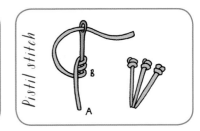

Pistil stitch

Bring the thread through the fabric at A. Holding the thread between your thumb and finger, wrap it around the needle two or three times.

Insert the needle into the fabric at B, making sure it's quite close to A. Push the needle through the fabric, carefully easing the knot off the needle. Pull the needle and remaining thread through the knot and fabric, then gently tug the thread to create a tight knot.

Keeping a good tension of the thread, take the needle down through B and pull the thread through to form a knot with a 'tail'.

Buttonhole wheel stitch

This stitch can be used in its own right as decoration – scattered or as a border. It can also be used as a filler.

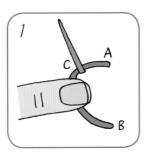

Start the stitch by pulling the needle up at A and then insert the needle at B in the centre. Pull it up at C, taking care to keep the needle inside the loop created – you can use your finger to keep the loop in place.

Continue in this way to complete the wheel.

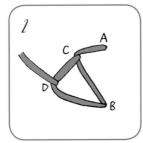

Insert the needle at B again, and pull it up at D to create the next spoke.

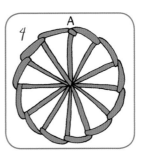

Fasten the last spoke of the wheel with a tiny straight stitch, joining at A. Take care to keep the tension quite tight, so the stitch doesn't loosen.

Using embroidery hoops

If you want to use an embroidery hoop, make sure it is large enough to fit in the motif comfortably. The large motifs are designed to fit inside a 15cm (6in) hoop, but you may find a 17.8cm (7in) size gives you a bit more room to work. The mini motifs fit in a 7.6cm (3in) hoop. Take care to have a sufficient length of fabric around the outside of the hoop to secure the motif.

You may wish to bind the inner hoop with special binding tape, as I have done here. This not only holds the fabric more firmly, but also helps to prevent the hoop from marking the fabric. Use a cotton twill tape that is 2.5cm (1in) wide, or if you can't find any, cut strips of spare fabric to a similar width.

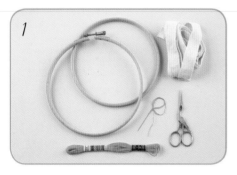

1 Assemble your items. You'll need a hoop, binding tape, a threaded needle and embroidery scissors.

2 Tightly wrap the binding tape all around your inner hoop.

3 Secure the tape to the inner hoop by oversewing the first and last bound sections together.

4 Place your embroidered piece over the bound inner ring, and then carefully push the outer ring over the top. You may need to loosen the screw a few times to adjust the tension of the fabric.

5 Once the design is firmly in between the hoops, turn your work over. Starting from the area near the screw, gently tug the fabric towards you and work your way around the hoop. Tighten the screw to finally secure your embroidered design.

To neatly finish off the back of your mandala, cut an approx. 2.5cm (1in) circular edge in the fabric around your hooped design, and glue the remaining fabric to the back of your work. If you prefer to cut your fabric before placing your mandala in the hoop, follow Using Dandelyne hoops steps 1–4 opposite.

14

Using Dandelyne hoops

The mini mandalas are designed to fit in a 5.5cm (2¼in) mini hoop by Dandelyne™ so they can be made into brooches and necklaces or even magnets. Dandelyne hoops can be bought online, either at dandelyne.com or through your local stockist's website; they may also be available in your local embroidery shop, so make sure to ask if they stock them. The mini hoops come with full instructions for assembly. These hoops are for display only, and can't be used as a regular embroidery hoop for stitching.

To work the mini mandalas for the mini hoops you will need to transfer the design to a piece of fabric that will fit either a 7.6cm (3in) or a 10cm (4in) regular hoop. Once you have embroidered the design you can then put it together with the mini hoop.

TIP
Glue a brooch fastener to your Dandelyne hoop to make a pretty brooch!

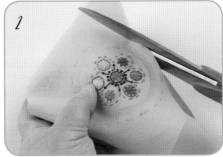

1 Place your Dandelyne hoop on your design and draw a dashed cutting line around the hoop, approx. 7mm (¼in) away.

4 Flip over your work and glue around the edge of the fabric. Push the fabric down in a circular motion.

2 Remove the hoop and cut away the excess fabric.

5 Add glue to the backing plate. Carefully position it on the back of the hoop, with the notch at the top near the screw. Press down and leave to dry.

3 Place the cut design onto the pale centre plate, then pop them into the mini hoop. Push down to secure and tighten the screw.

6 Your finished mini mandala in a hoop!

The mandalas

For each embroidered mandala you will find the following: a colour diagram, a stitch key and 'colour beans' which show the number of each DMC thread colour used. Find a particular stitch in the diagram, then pick the colour from the 'beans'. One note about the diagrams: where chain stitch has been used, it is a thicker line in the diagram than the rest, but in the transfer sheet it is the same thickness. This is to make sure that it will be covered by the embroidery.

The embroideries on the following pages are inspiration for how you can stitch the mandala motifs in this book. At the back of the book you will find iron-on transfer sheets for all of the mandalas.

Two of the embroidered mandalas (Scheherazade's Garden on page 24, Pastel Bouquet on page 26) have more stitching than you will find in their transfer sheets. This is to give you the opportunity to add your own favourite stitches. However, if you would like to stitch them exactly like the sample embroideries, simply follow the information in the diagrams.

I hope that you will see the embroidered versions as ideas or starting points for your own mandala creations. Use completely different colours, thicker thread or different stitches in your pieces – the possibilities are endless.

Getting started

Six-stranded cotton embroidery thread may be the obvious choice for many projects but there are many other types of thread available to experiment with, such as crewel wool, perle cotton and metallic threads. All the embroideries in the book have been worked with two strands of DMC embroidery thread.

If you intend to use your mandalas to embellish clothes or accessories, there is a huge variety of fabrics you can stitch on: linen, cotton, denim, felt and even knit fabrics. Some fabrics, such as jersey or very fine fabrics, may need a stabilizer to make them easy to stitch on. When choosing fabrics and threads for your projects, it is a good idea to keep the end use in mind. If the project will need frequent washing and ironing, for example, you may want to prewash the fabric to avoid shrinkage after you have embroidered it.

It may be a good idea to stitch a small sampler to test the colour fastness of the threads you want to use, especially if using special or hand-dyed threads. Not all threads stand up to washing so bear this in mind when making your selection. Metallics or wool, for example, will not work well for items that will need frequent washing, but they can be washed by hand in cold water. Check the guidelines from the manufacturer when using special threads.

Before you start stitching, prepare your fabric by pressing it to get rid of creases. Raw edges can be hemmed or trimmed with pinking shears to reduce fraying.

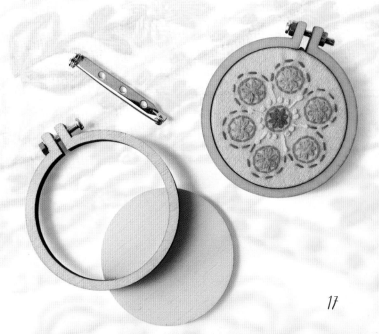

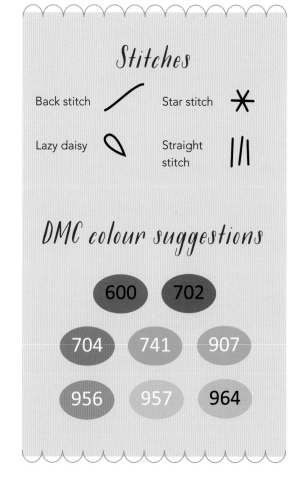

1

Sakura Clusters

Admire the beauty of the cherry blossoms as they bloom briefly in spring. A celebration of the renewal of life, but a reminder too of how ephemeral life is. Add more star stitches to create mini clusters among the flowers.

Stitches

Back stitch	/	Star stitch	✳
Lazy daisy	◯	Straight stitch	|||

DMC colour suggestions

600 702

704 741 907

956 957 964

Stitching suggestions ...
Start the embroidery with the stems and branches, then move through the leaves and flowers, finishing with the stars.

2

Rainbow Orbit

In this imaginary Solar System, you can begin with the star in the centre, and then work your way outwards, or start with the circles and then add the other stitches. Maybe savour working one colour at a time before moving on to the next.

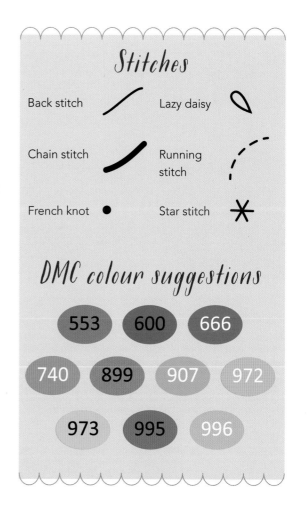

Stitches

Back stitch		Lazy daisy
Chain stitch		Running stitch
French knot	●	Star stitch ✳

DMC colour suggestions

553	600	666
740	899	907	972
973	995	996

Stitching suggestions ...

Work the continuous stitches first: back stitch, chain stitch and running stitch. Then, move onto the rows of individual stitches: French knot, lazy daisy and star.

3

Bloom Coil

Colourful flowers in pairs of opposites are inspired by the colour wheel, using primary and secondary colours. The embroidery has been worked in back stitch, with a sprinkling of lazy daisy stitch. By keeping the number of stitches simple, you can enjoy the quiet mindfulness of focusing on the stitches for each leaf or petal.

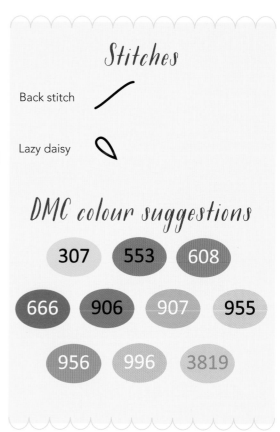

Stitching suggestions ...

Stitch one pair of complimentary-colour flowers at a time, starting with the flower bud and then working the branch, the leaves and ending with the spirals. Finish the embroidery with the lazy daisy flowers.

Stitches

Back stitch

Lazy daisy

DMC colour suggestions

307 553 608

666 906 907 955

956 996 3819

4

Scheherazade's Garden

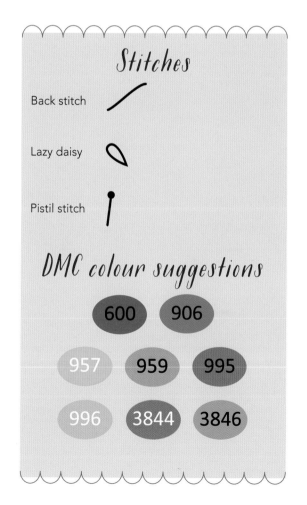

This secret garden, shaded by palm trees and cooled by numerous fountains, is a quiet place to think while adding extra stitches of your choice.

Stitches

Back stitch

Lazy daisy

Pistil stitch

DMC colour suggestions

600   906

957   959   995

996   3844   3846

Stitching suggestions ...

Starting from the middle, work all the back stitches first, and then add the lazy daisy and pistil stitches.

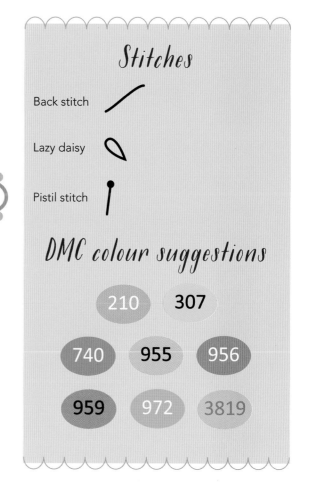

5

Pastel Bouquet

This spring-time bouquet has extra room in the transfer for embellishing the flowers and the large hearts. In the stitched version, pistil stitches have been added, but lazy daisy stitches or French knots would be equally pretty.

Stitches

Back stitch	/
Lazy daisy	⬮
Pistil stitch	╷

DMC colour suggestions

210   307

740   955   956

959   972   3819

Stitching suggestions ...
Stitch the branches first then add the leaves and the large hearts. Work the flowers next, and then finish the embroidery with the small hearts.

6

Paisley Constellation

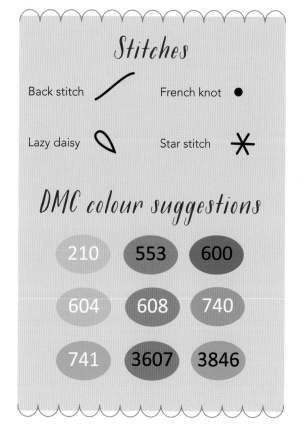

There may not be an actual Paisley Constellation, but you can still let your mind wander to wonder about the stars and the galaxies that surround us and make us. We are all beautiful stardust.

Stitches

Back stitch ╱   French knot ●

Lazy daisy ◗   Star stitch ✳

DMC colour suggestions

210	553	600
604	608	740
741	3607	3846

Stitching suggestions ...

Work the outlines of the paisleys first, then add the scalloped edges. Stitch the other back stitch sections, then work the flowers and leaves. Add the French knots, stars and lazy daisy stitches. Finish the embroidery with the stars in between the paisleys.

7

Poinsettia Flourish

In this embroidery, metallic thread has been used to add a bit of sparkle. The way metallic thread catches the light is very pretty, but working with this thread requires patience. Metallic thread twists and knots more than regular six-stranded thread. To avoid this, use a short length of thread, about 20cm (8in) long. Use a thread conditioner to help tame the thread.

Stitching suggestions ...

Starting with the green leaves in the centre, work each 'round' of the same shape at a time before moving on to the next. When all the back stitches are done, add the fly stitches.

Stitches

Back stitch ╱

Fly stitch ╲╱

DMC colour suggestions

| 600 | 666 |
| 702 | E3852 |

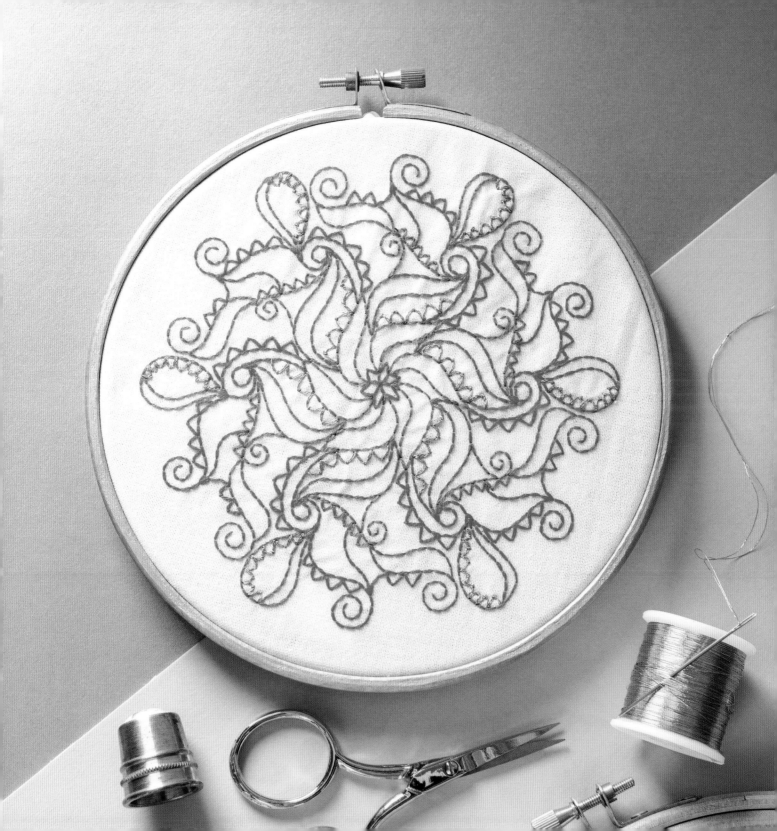

8

Winter Solstice

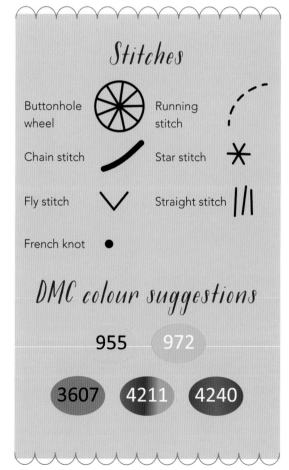

In this motif you can really get lost in the repetition of stitches. Stitch one row at a time, gradually, giving yourself space to relax and be calm as you stitch. When working the pistil stitches and buttonhole wheels, be mindful of the tension of the stitches.

Stitches

Buttonhole wheel	⊛	Running stitch	
Chain stitch	／	Star stitch	✳
Fly stitch	∨	Straight stitch	❘❘❘
French knot	•		

DMC colour suggestions

955   972

3607   4211   4240

Stitching suggestions ...

Work the continuous stitches first: chain stitch and running stitch. Then, move onto the rows of individual stitches: French knot, pistil stitch, lazy daisy, fly stitch, straight stitch, buttonhole wheel and star.

9

Cerulean Petals

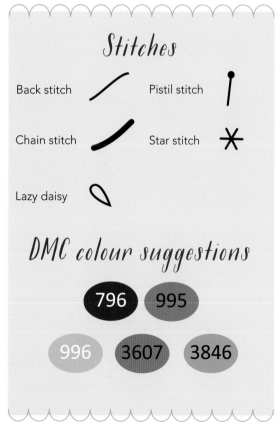

This design has been inspired by how the morning light catches on the sempervivums in my garden. It highlights the shape of the petals, nature's own mandala. Some of the petals have been left unadorned so there is room to add more stitches if you like.

Stitches

Back stitch	╱	Pistil stitch	●
Chain stitch	╱	Star stitch	✳
Lazy daisy	◗		

DMC colour suggestions

796 995 996 3607 3846

Stitching suggestions ...
Work the chain stitch sections first, then add the back stitch sections. Finish with lazy daisy, pistil and start stitches.

10

Atomic Burst

The variegated thread in this mandala is a type called Coloris, where the colour changes are more dramatic than regular variegated thread. It is like using multiple colours at once, and creates a beautiful effect.

Stitching suggestions ...

Start with the large leaves in the centre, then stitch the outlines in back stitch. Work the flowers, and then finish by adding French knots, fly stitch and lazy daisy stitch.

Stitches

Back stitch /   French knot ●

Fly stitch ∨   Straight stitch | | |

Lazy daisy ⟋

DMC colour suggestions

600   604

741   956   4507

11

Friendship Meadow

This mandala is a celebration of friendship – of those friends who lift us up and believe in us no matter what. Wander in the tall grasses and gather armfuls of friendship flowers in every colour.

Stitches

Back stitch   ╱

Lazy daisy   ◯

Star stitch   ✳

DMC colour suggestions

666   740   906

956   959   973   995

996   3607   3819

Stitching suggestions ...

Start the embroidery with the stems, then add the large and small leaves and the flower bud at the end. Finish the embroidery with the star stitches and the small lazy daisy flowers.

Floral Perch

Birds are perched between the branches of flowering trees. Let these heralds of spring inspire you to use a pulchritude of vibrant colours.

Stitching suggestions ...

Work through the branches and leaves first, then add the flower perches and birds. Finish the embroidery with the French knots.

Stitches

Back stitch ╱

Fly stitch ╲╱

French knot ●

DMC colour suggestions

553 740 956

973 3846

The Explorers

From the familiar to the exotic, the very close to the very far away, explorers move our minds and hearts; whether its through the tiniest atom or when they're floating above our home planet.

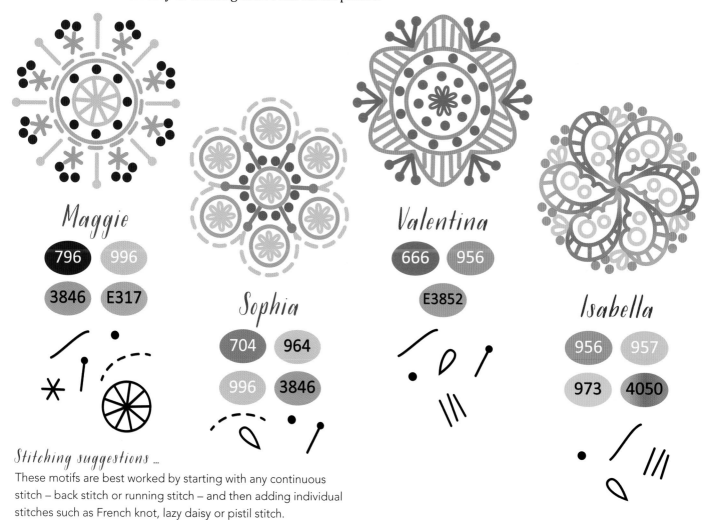

Maggie

796 996
3846 E317

Sophia

704 964
996 3846

Valentina

666 956
E3852

Isabella

956 957
973 4050

Stitching suggestions ...

These motifs are best worked by starting with any continuous stitch – back stitch or running stitch – and then adding individual stitches such as French knot, lazy daisy or pistil stitch.

The Gardeners

These mandalas celebrate life in the garden: the seeds we sow and the flowers we grow; the animals that make it home, and the birds that fly to and fro.

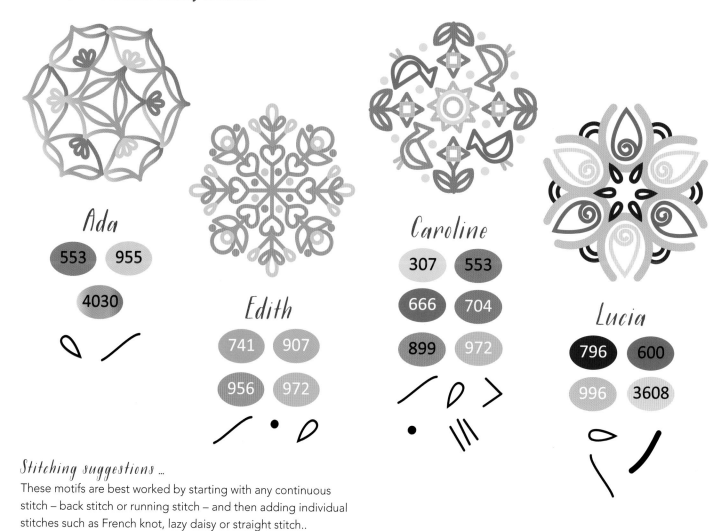

Ada

553   955

4030

Edith

741   907

956   972

Caroline

307   553

666   704

899   972

Lucia

796   600

996   3608

Stitching suggestions ...

These motifs are best worked by starting with any continuous stitch – back stitch or running stitch – and then adding individual stitches such as French knot, lazy daisy or straight stitch..

44

The Artists

Find your inner artist in these bold and colourful mandalas.
Let their energy be your inspiration for colour and pattern.

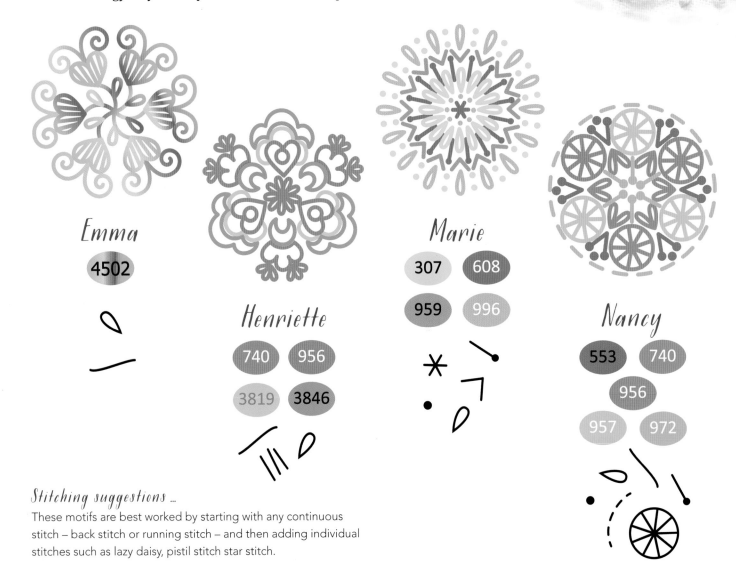

Emma

4502

Henriette

740 956

3819 3846

Marie

307 608

959 996

Nancy

553 740

956

957 972

Stitching suggestions ...

These motifs are best worked by starting with any continuous
stitch – back stitch or running stitch – and then adding individual
stitches such as lazy daisy, pistil stitch star stitch.

Transferring the designs

You can transfer the mandala designs using the transfer sheets on the following pages. Each one corresponds with the sampler numbers on pages 18–47, and can be used up to ten times. When cutting out the mini mandalas, take care to leave as much paper as possible around each motif.

When you have used a transfer, store it in the pocket on the back cover to keep it safe until you wish to use it again. Transfer the motifs using an ordinary iron (without steam) set on 'cotton'. Only use on fabrics that won't be damaged by the heat of the iron. If possible, test the fabric first.

The transfers work best on light-coloured fabrics; for darker colours you may wish to use the alternative method explained below.

Please note that the transfer ink will fade from the fabric when washed but may not disappear completely; when stitching, make sure you follow the lines closely to ensure the ink is hidden beneath the embroidery.

Alternatively, if you prefer not to use an iron, you can transfer a motif by photocopying a design, taping the printed design to a window, securing your fabric on top of this and then tracing the design using a water soluble pen or a stylus. For darker fabrics, a white transfer paper can be used. Place the transfer paper with the transfer side facing down onto the fabric, place the printed design on top and trace it using a water soluble pen or a stylus.

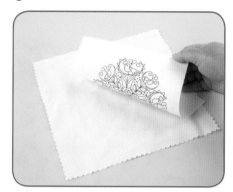

1 Cut out the transfer design you wish to use. Iron the fabric, then place the transfer with the ink side facing down on the right side of your fabric.

2 Place the iron over the transfer area and press down for about ten seconds. Make sure not to move the iron as this may blur the motif.

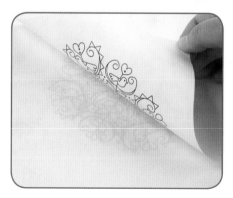

3 Carefully lift a corner of the transfer to make sure it has printed on the fabric. If not, leave the iron for a little longer or increase the temperature and try again. When the motif has successfully been transferred to the fabric, remove the transfer and place the fabric in a hoop ready for stitching.

13

14

15

16

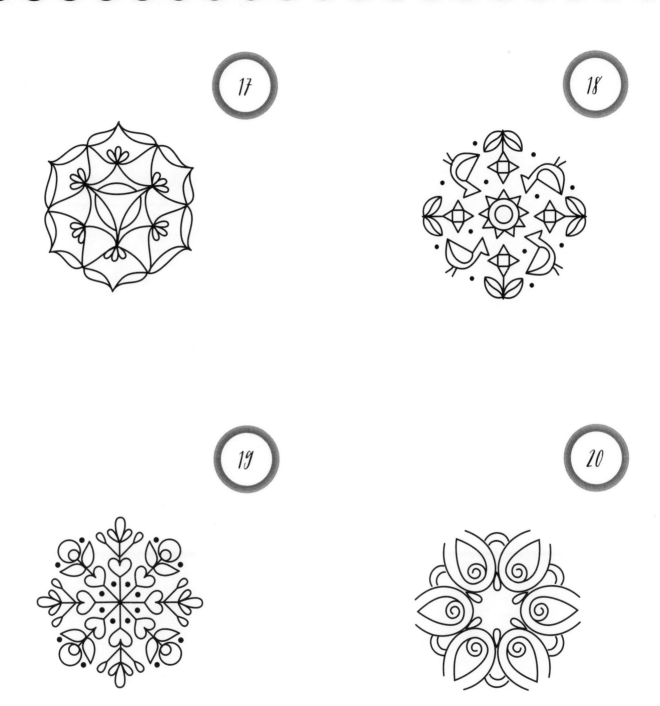

17

18

19

20

21

22

23

24

Aurora Floret

Lose yourself in your stitching with this final hidden mandala.
Transfer Aurora Floret onto your chosen piece of fabric, sew the
basic outlines in back stitch or chain stitch, then start experimenting
– add stars, flowers or other shapes to make your own unique motif.